Text by Julia Stone
Illustrations copyright © 2009 Dubravka Kolanovic
This edition copyright © 2015 Lion Hudson

The right of Dubravka Kolanovic to be identified as the illustrator of this work has been asserted
by her in accordance with the Copyright, Designs and Patents Act 1988.

Published by Lion Children's Books
an imprint of
**Lion Hudson plc**
Wilkinson House, Jordan Hill Road,
Oxford OX2 8DR, England
www.lionhudson.com/lionchildrens

ISBN 978 0 7459 7610 5

First edition 2015

A catalogue record for this book is available from the British Library

Printed and bound in Malaysia, June 2015, LH18

# The Christmas Story
## for Little Angels

Julia Stone ✳ Dubravka Kolanovic

LION
CHILDREN'S

The story of Christmas is the story of Baby Jesus.

It all happened long ago, in a country far away.

There, in a town called Nazareth, lived a woman named Mary.

One day, as she was busy with everyday things, an angel appeared.

"Oh!" Mary was startled.

"Don't be afraid," said the angel.
"God has chosen you for something very special.
You are to be the mother of his Son.
You will name him 'Jesus'.
He will show the world
God's love."

Mary smiled and shook her head.

"I can't be a mother yet," she said. "I'm not yet married."

"Whatever God wants can come true," said the angel. "Will you be part of God's plan?"

Mary knew at once: "Yes, I will," she said.

The angel disappeared back to heaven.

Mary walked out among the springtime flowers.

"I really truly believe that everything will work out," she said to herself. "I know I can trust in God's promises.

"I have never felt so happy."

Even so, there was one fairly big problem.

Everything had been arranged for Mary to marry Joseph.

When he heard that Mary was expecting a baby, he felt very sad.

"It's not my baby," he sighed. "Perhaps I should call off the wedding."

In a dream, an angel spoke to him.

"God has a special plan for you," said the angel. "God has chosen you to look after Mary and her baby. He is God's own Son, and he will show God's love to all the world."

Now Joseph felt happy too.

He went to find Mary.

"I want us still to be married," he said. "Now, this is what we should do next.

"The emperor who rules our country wants to count just how many people there are.

"I need to go to the town where my family come from, to put my name on the list.

"That means Bethlehem. And I want you to come too, because we are going to be husband and wife."

Together Mary and Joseph made the long journey to
Bethlehem. It was now almost time for the baby to be born.

"I shall be glad when we get there," said Mary. "I really
want to lie down somewhere soft and comfortable."

"We're sure to find a place to stay," said Joseph.
    But they couldn't. By the time Mary and Joseph reached
Bethlehem, all the rooms were full.

Who knows how they found even a stable to shelter in.
Perhaps it was the donkey who led them there, sniffing
the sweet hay in a manger.

There, Mary's baby Jesus was born.

She wrapped him snugly in swaddling clothes.

Even the animals in the stable seemed to stop their
scuffling and munching to come close and see.

Out on the hills nearby, shepherds had gathered around a fire. They needed to stay awake through the night, to make sure their sheep were safe.

All kinds of wild animals prowled in the dark.

Was that a fox they could hear? Or a wolf?

All of a sudden, the night sky turned to gold.
    It was as if someone had pulled back a curtain, and the
shepherds could see all the way to heaven.

Out of the golden shining, an angel spoke.

"I have the very best news!" cried the angel. "Tonight, in Bethlehem, a baby has been born. He is God's own Son, and he will show God's love to all the world."

All around came the sound of angels singing.

Then everything was dark, as before.

   The shepherds looked at each other in amazement, then…

   "Come on!" said one. "Let's go to Bethlehem and see!"

They hurried along the quiet streets until they saw a room where a light was shining.

Inside they found Mary and Joseph and the newborn baby.

"Everything is just as the angel said," they explained. "This baby must truly be God's special baby – God's promised king."

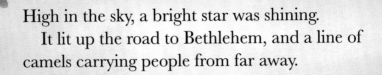

High in the sky, a bright star was shining.
It lit up the road to Bethlehem, and a line of
camels carrying people from far away.

Among them were wise men
who looked for meaning in the
patterns of the stars.
"The new star is a sign," they
agreed. "It tells us that a king
has been born.
"Perhaps we will find him in
Bethlehem."

The star stopped at the very place where Jesus was.

The wise men brought out their gifts: gold, frankincense, and myrrh.

And even the littlest camel boy understood:

Here indeed was God's chosen king. He would show the world God's love, and welcome people into God's own kingdom.